To Rys

VEGANS
IN
ICELAND

With love & best wishes.

PROUDLY SUPPORTING
SEA SHEPHERD

Sales of this book
support the work of
Sea Shepherd in Iceland.

www.seashepherdglobal.org

First published in 2020 by
Jonathan Straight Limited / Artbukz

Copyright © Jonathan Straight Limited 2019
jonathan@planetstraight.com

ISBN 978-1-8380657-0-6

10 9 8 7 6 5 4 3 2 1

Design and production management by Abi Read Studio
holla@abi-read.com

Printed and bound by Gomer Press
www.gomer.co.uk

VEGANS IN ICELAND

JONATHAN STRAIGHT FRSA

www.vegansiniceland.com

CONTENTS

'Prior to visiting Iceland, my perception was of a lonely, harsh and barren place.'

JONATHAN STRAIGHT | PHOTOGRAPHER

VEGANS IN ICELAND

Prior to visiting Iceland, my perception was of a lonely, harsh and barren place. Somewhere that was permanently dark for long periods of the year. A place where nothing grows and everyone is wholly dependent on what can be brought in by sea or by air.

And what would people eat in such a place? My thoughts turned to whale blubber and other such horrors. What if one were a vegan here? Were there actually any vegans in Iceland? What would they eat and how would they survive? Surely, to be a vegan in such a place would require extreme dedication and attention. It would be difficult and would only be achievable by a committed hardcore group of people.

It was a novel by Hallgrímur Helgason that first got me interested in Iceland. *The Hitman's Guide to Housecleaning* was a fabulous and entertaining read. It was promoted on the shelves in a bookshop I visited, and I gladly took up their recommendation. I followed it with one of his other novels, *101 Reykjavík,* which although I thought was not a patch on the later book, made me very keen to visit the City and see it for myself. As a street photographer, I was interested in documenting what I thought would be interesting characters. But, as a vegan, what would I eat there?

I found a page on Facebook called Vegan Travellers to Iceland. My question was quickly replied to by Vigga þórðar who sent me pages and pages of information about where vegan food could be found across Iceland. Vigga also invited me to photograph the Cube of Truth. At that time, I didn't know what this was, so I asked. I wondered if there was more to know about the Icelandic vegan community and so I asked about this too. Ten short biographies of people I should meet came back. Here was the beginning of a project.

Having landed at Keflavík Airport, picking up the obligatory 4x4, I drove across a stark, volcanic landscape. It was a drab and rainy day with dark, low-hanging clouds. It looked surreal and somewhat disturbing. Perhaps my preconceptions were true?

Arriving in Reykjavík, my first job was to photograph the Cube of Truth, my Leica in one hand and an umbrella in the other.

But the next day, the weather changed. It was a balmy 20 degrees, about as good as it gets. There was hardly any darkness at night, and I was warmly welcomed by all of the people I met. People suggested other people, and so the project evolved. Far from struggling, there is excellent vegan produce in all of the main

supermarkets and a lot of restaurants provide vegan food. I even found a few exclusively vegan establishments, including a vegan gay bar.

This collection of portraits and brief biographies shows the diversity of the Icelandic vegan community and the many different routes people have followed to come to veganism – something that unites them all in a small country where there are very few degrees of separation.

If there is a message in this book, it is that the vegan way of life is spreading and gaining massive momentum, and many of those that supply the food we consume are open to facilitating this change. If there can be a thriving vegan community in Iceland, then surely, there can be the same anywhere.

Jonathan Straight FRSA
July 2019

Exit to Iceland

CUBE OF TRUTH

Each Sunday afternoon, a small group of vegan activists assembles on the Laugavegur, the main street in downtown Reykjavík. They put up a portable tent without sides and then each person puts a Guy Fawkes mask on. They stand back-to-back, with flat-screen televisions harnessed to their bodies, powered by a battery that sits on the ground between them.

The screens show scenes of animal cruelty from slaughterhouses. While this is happening, others wearing clothes bearing the Anonymous for the Voiceless brand engage with passers-by, advocating a vegan lifestyle. They seem to be generally well-received and have been successful in converting people to being vegan.

CUBE OF TRUTH

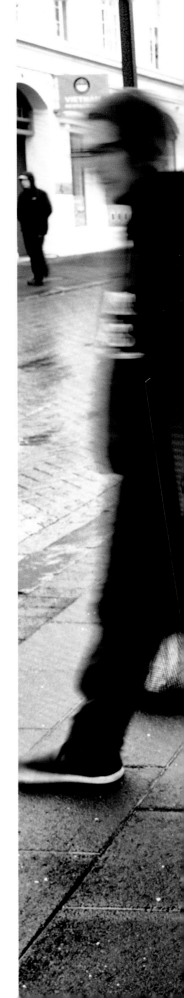

The screens
show scenes of
animal cruelty from
slaughterhouses.
While this is
happening, others
engage with passers-
by, advocating a
vegan lifestyle.

When not standing under the tent, activists remove their masks and wear them on the shoulder.

» Sædís Karen Stefánsdóttir Walker
Laugavegur, Reykjavík

VEGAN BODY IMAGE

Sædís has been bullied in the past. She has been told that she is not a worthy individual because she is considered overweight. Until a few years ago, she believed the jibes but was aware of women becoming more confident and being unapologetic about simply being themselves. This inspired her and gave her the strength to slowly increase her self-confidence.

The bullying led to eating disorders; she would not eat for days and then would binge. She describes her relationship with food as having been compromised.

This all changed in 2017 when Sædís became vegan. She says that she stopped being afraid of food. Stopping consuming cruelty meant that cruelty no longer consumed her. She says that she was eating to feel good and healthy regardless of what her weight might be.

Sædís believes that fat people are oppressed in the same way that animals are and that as a victim of oppression, she cannot imagine oppressing others. She would like to write a book on this theme and to this end is currently doing a BA in English, focusing on literature and writing.

» **Solla Eiriks**
Glo Restaurant, Reykjavík

VEGAN PIONEER

Solla was named after her grandmother, a lady who moved to Copenhagen in 1915 to study nursing. There, she joined a vegetarian movement led by the Swiss, raw food pioneer, Dr Maximilian Bircher-Benner. Adopting a raw and mostly vegan diet, her grandmother moved back to Iceland. There, she began working with the Naturopathic Society of Iceland to encourage the adoption of this diet from a health perspective.

Living on Vestmannaeyjar, an archipelago off the south coast of Iceland, she was quite self-sufficient, developing skills in sprouting, preserving and fermenting foods. Solla senior then moved back to the mainland in order to educate her son, who became, Solla's father. Meanwhile, Solla's mother had become vegetarian at 12 years old and grew her own food at the family's summerhouse. Both parents are now well into their 80s and are still mostly self-sufficient.

Solla herself is allergic to all animal protein and was brought up with a mostly vegetarian diet. At 17, she too

WELCOME TO GLÓ
A HEALTHY EATING
VEGAN RESTAURANT
WITH ATTITUDE

gló
vegan

Wi Fi

moved to Copenhagen, following the journey of her grandmother, where she met a naturopath who helped with her allergies. The strict diet he recommended cured her symptoms, and it was at this stage she became vegan.

In 1984, she moved back to Iceland and worked as a textile designer while giving classes in making tofu and other vegan foods that were not available on the market at the time, such as plant milks. This led to her opening the first vegan restaurant in Iceland in 1994. It was a great success and was spurned on by her knowledge of raw and living food gained from a trip to Puerto Rico.

That restaurant was sold in 2005 and Solla went to California to study gourmet raw cuisine, which became very popular. She catered the wedding for raw food advocate, David Woolfe and subsequently spoke at conferences organised by him. Over the years, she has catered for many famous people

including the Beckhams, Gwyneth Paltrow and Neil Young.

2010 saw Solla taking over the Glo Restaurant as the owners wanted to concentrate on their yoga business. At that time, it was serving meat with vegetables and salads, but Solla made it mostly vegan. The business has grown with four other branches and investors. The other branches still serve meat, but the Klapparstígur branch in Reykjavík (coincidentally on the same site as the original offices of the Naturopathic Society of Iceland) is now completely vegan. Solla also has her own 100% vegan and organic food line – Himmeskt – which is sold in many of Iceland's supermarkets.

More recently, all of these business interests have been sold off, and Solla is looking forward to completing her contract with the new owners at which point she will be free to continue her vegan food adventures.

VEGAN PIONEER

» **Sigríður Ýr Unnarsdóttir**
Glerárlón, Akureyri

VEGAN ADVENTURES

Sigríður is a world record holder having travelled more than 1500 miles on a pocket bicycle. Her name means victory in Norse, which is very appropriate. It also means beautiful, which is appropriate too. Sigríður is not someone you will easily forget.

Her day job is as an adventure guide. She will take you on an expedition to a glacier, climbing up ice, or kayaking if you prefer. But more recently she has started working with paddleboards, specifically, teaching yoga while on a paddleboard in a pond. Called SUP yoga, this is very difficult, requiring additional strength and flexibility to maintain balance.

Sigríður started her plant-based journey as a vegetarian but was converted to being vegan by a friend after just one month. Now in her fifth year as a vegan, she has relocated from Reykjavík to the northern town of Akureyri.

Sigríður is a world record holder having travelled more than 1500 miles on a pocket bicycle. Her name means victory in Norse, which is very appropriate.

WASTE-FREE VEGAN

Amanda is a member of Sea Shepherd, a marine conservation organisation. They are against all things that can be damaging to the oceans, including plastic pollution and hunting. In Iceland, this is particularly relevant, as whales are sometimes hunted for their meat.

Sea Shepherd is somewhat controversial in Iceland, as activists sank two whaling boats in 1986 and some of the local population have not forgiven them for this. Nonetheless, Amanda is the local Chapter Leader and takes part in peaceful activities such as beach clean-ups, political lobbying and sharing graphic information on social media.

She became vegetarian aged 17, having made the connection between the animals she loved and the meat she was eating. Initially, she had to cook for herself, finally becoming vegan in 2017.

WASTE-FREE VEGAN

« **Dispensing liquid soap into a recycled jar**
Vistvera plastic-free store, Reykjavík

At the time, Amanda did not know any other vegans and found her diet inconvenienced family and friends.

Taking her own food to family gatherings, something interesting happened. Everyone else began to eat her food. Other vegans were found on social media, and Amanda began to volunteer for the Cube of Truth.

Now one of the organisers in Iceland, she gets people to reach their own conclusions about veganism by asking carefully-phrased questions and by being friendly.

This was just the beginning. Amanda began to consume less and recycle more, living a low waste lifestyle and advocating for this too. Amanda's life is a reflection of her belief in reducing environmental impact and suffering. Her influence is now growing and spreading through her activism.

VEGAN FOOTBALL

⌃ **Club logo painted on gymnasium wall**

Beggi plays in defence for the First Division Icelandic team, Fjölnir, based in Grafarvogur, a residential district of Reykjavík. They topped the league in 2016 along with another team. He has been vegan since 2015.

It was his vegan girlfriend who prompted him to make the change. He claims to have watched and listened and as an aspiring professional footballer, felt that a vegan diet might help with energy levels and recovery times.

He says that veganism is growing in its stature, and since he became vegan, he can find something to eat in almost any restaurant.

His recovery times are now much improved. His health and the environment are also motivating factors, but the benefit to his sport ranks in first place.

VEGAN FOOTBALL

'My health and the environment are also motivating factors, but the benefit to my sport ranks in first place.'

BEGGI | FOOTBALLER

» **Hulda B. Waage**
Kraftlyftingafélag Akureyrar, Akureyri

VEGAN WEIGHTS

Hulda is an Icelandic champion powerlifter. She has been lifting weights since 2011, becoming vegan shortly afterwards. Her success was immediate, making her the first vegan to win the National Cup.

As long as she eats well, being vegan has been no detriment to her performance, and she feels it may well be an advantage. Training hard each day in a gym with loud thrash metal playing, she binds her legs, tightens her belt and lifts some astounding weights. Following this, she bench-presses some immense weights too.

While her family are not all vegans, she only cooks vegan food, regularly sharing her skills on social media. They can take it or leave it, she says, but her youngest daughter is now following in her mother's footsteps.

Her best squat lift is 245kg which is three times the author's weight!

⌄ Squat lift
Kraftlyftingafélag Akureyrar, Akureyri

» **Ragnar Freyr**
Klapparstígur, Reykjavík

VEGAN APP

Graphic designer, Ragnar, is a vegan activist who takes part in the Cube of Truth most weeks. He has created an app called Vegan Iceland. This lists all the restaurants in Iceland that offer vegan options clearly mentioned on the menu. At the time of writing, there were 160 establishments listed and another 60 waiting to be included.

He considers the app an act of activism as some places will not openly list their vegan dishes for fear of reprisals. This app persuades them to demonstrate their commitment to the vegan cause. More than 3,500 users have downloaded the app, which was created with his business partner, a political activist.

Ragnar became a vegetarian nine years ago and has been vegan for six years. It was his pet dog who was the catalyst as he began comparing the dog to piglets. Raised on a farm, he was the first generation to move to the City, and he knew he had to be vegan having done some online research about the effects of dairy foods. Since becoming vegan, his high blood pressure and sleep apnoea have both gone away.

Vegan

'I consider listing
these restaurants
on my app an
act of activism,
as some places will
not openly list their
vegan dishes for
fear of reprisals.'

RAGNAR | GRAPHIC DESIGNER

VEGAN APP

VEGAN YOGA

Tinna is an Icelandic native. Her husband, Jacob, hails from the United States. They share their passion for plant-based foods and yoga with people from all over the globe. They recently managed a yoga retreat centre in Mexico, but then decided to move to Akureyri in Iceland, because they saw a great need for their knowledge and experience in the far north of the country.

Tinna had experienced various health issues until encouraged by a coach to drop animal products. Since being plant-based for almost three years, she describes the changes as dramatic, eventually leading her studying to be a raw food plant-based chef.

Jacob grew up as a vegetarian under the influence of his family. Unbeknown to him, he was lactose intolerant. After kicking dairy, improvements to his health were evident. One thing he finds challenging in Iceland is the lack of abundant, organic greens. When these are in the shops, they buy loads of them and then freeze or dehydrate them for future use.

Tinna and Jacob are inspired individuals with a mission to inspire others through healthy eating, movement, and mindful practices.

⌃ **Yoga position**

VEGAN ENTREPRENEUR

» Sæunn Ingibjörg Marinósdóttir
Veganmatur warehouse, Hafnarfjörður

VEGAN ENTREPRENEUR

Sæunn is a founder of the Icelandic Vegan Society which is now called by the name Grænkeri. Grænkeri is the correct word in Icelandic for vegan, but it is a relatively new word and so the English - vegan - is more commonly used.

Her company, Veganmatur, is one of the key importers of vegan food into Iceland. She also has a food production business and owns a fast food outlet, Jömm. Veganmatur has been established for seven years and is the only fully vegan wholesaler and distributor in Iceland. Due to this business and her activism, Sæunn has a unique understanding of the market.

This all started with her husband importing Oumph! a meat substitute from Sweden, as a side hustle. At the time, Sæunn was working in the Glo

vegan restaurant in Reykjavík.
As things grew, they both began to
work full time on this enterprise.
They have two business partners who
are also vegan, and they choose their
suppliers very carefully based on their
ethical performance.

As well as importing and producing
food, Sæunn owns the wonderful Jömm
fast food store which is now based in
the food court in the Kringlan Mall in
Reykjavík. Here, wraps and burgers are
available, primarily made from Oumph!
and augmented with their own range
of home-made sauces.

Salads, sandwiches and ready meals
are produced each day for distribution
around Iceland, and they have a shop,
Vegan Búðin, in Hafnarfjörður, which
opens on Saturdays selling carefully-
curated vegan foodstuffs as well as
some vegan clothing.

While Sæunn embodies a young
entrepreneur and runs a for-profit
business, she has defined social values
which also play a key role. She sees
her business as a form of activism with
the power to change the world for the
better. With 49% of Icelanders aged
18-29 either giving up meat or thinking
about it, her business seems set to
continue its meteoric rise.

VEGAN ENTREPRENEUR

VEFVERSLUN Á VEGANBUDIN.I

'I see my business as a form of activism with the power to change the world for the better.'

SÆUNN | ENTREPRENEUR

VEGAN ENTREPRENEUR

VEGAN HERMIT

Thor, real name Þórhallur, lives in a wooden shack literally in the middle of nowhere. He is about an hour out of Reykjavík; the final five miles of the journey are along a dirt track.

His dwelling place is not a legally adopted property, and it is very small. He has one room and sleeps above his kitchen area. Hot water comes straight from the ground in the mountains. This water is not potable and does not smell very nice.

Thor studies ethnology and also works with people who have learning disabilities and mental health issues. Each year, he acts as a security officer for the Reykjavík Pride Parade - an event that can last for several days.

He does travel into the City for work so gets the best of both worlds, but loves the serenity of being completely alone once the day has ended and he is cosy in his home.

VEGAN ACTIVISM

'I was called Maria' is written on a small adhesive label. Activist Stella has lots of labels with several different names on them, but the message is the same - a piece of meat is part of an animal which is now personified.

She rummages in the fridges and freezers in the Krónan Granda supermarket in Reykjavík, surreptitiously applying these stickers to packs of meat.

The intention is that the person buying the product might think long and hard about their purchase and indeed may not buy the product as a consequence.

This time she is spotted. The labels are all removed by shop staff, and she is thrown out. But she will be back another day.

⌃ 'I was called Maria'.
Pack of meat with activist label applied

Oumph! A popular vegan meat substitute imported from Sweden
Krónan Granda, Reykjavík

VEGAN SEX

Stella is a former sex worker who had lived in Iceland for three years at the time this was written. Prior to this, she lived in Sweden but was actually born in Greece. Describing herself as a love immigrant, Stella had already broken up with her partner by the time she arrived in Reykjavík. She is now running the Icelandic chapter of Sea Shepherd.

Her prior work offered a niche service, sometimes involving domination and occasionally the penetration of clients, at least four of whom were converted to being vegan. As may be expected, she claims to have had some strange experiences. That said, she says her clients were always much more respectful to her than her bosses or customers in her previous roles as a barista, translator, ghostwriter and professional dancer. She could choose who to work with and decline a booking if anyone was remotely disrespectful – a level of freedom not experienced in any other job she had done.

As a vegan activist with hundreds of hours of activism under her belt, Stella also campaigns against plastic in the environment, often stopping to pick up trash in the street that might cause harm to wildlife.

⌃ **Stella Anton**
Radisson Blu Saga Hotel, Reykjavík

VEGAN SEX

Stella is standing by the remains of two whaling vessels which were sunk by Sea Shepherd activists in 1986. These boats are now moored at the hidden and secluded beach of a fjord by the only whaling factory in Iceland.

VEGAN POLITICS

Vala is involved with local government as a politician within the Pirate Party. They are an anti-corruption movement.

She describes how four families own almost everything in Iceland and are very influential. The Minister of Finance is actually from the wealthiest family in the Country. A new constitution was agreed in 2012 which was supposed to temper this, but it has not yet been implemented. Vala believes that democracy in Iceland is faulty.

As an activist, Vala is vice chairman of the Vegan Society of Iceland and has organised protests against whaling in the past. She became vegetarian at 12 years old, both for ethical reasons and out of caring for animals. First hearing about veganism about ten years ago, she did not immediately see the point. But when a friend's baby tragically passed

When a friend's baby tragically passed away and her friend was still lactating, she shared her empathy with dairy cows, and this opened Vala's eyes to veganism.

away and her friend was still lactating, she shared her empathy with dairy cows, and this opened Vala's eyes to veganism. She did Veganuary and never looked back.

As well as being a politician, activist and labour union organiser, Vala is also a talented DJ and the owner of feminist event management group, Puzzy Patrol. She particularly enjoys playing female hip hop and funk at local clubs and has organised concerts and gigs with female artists, for example, at the Iceland Airwaves festival.

» **Alda Villiljós**
Curious, Hafnarstræti, Reykjavík

LGBT VEGAN

Alda is an LGBT activist running their own vegan baking business. They supply local bars and restaurants with vegan baked goods. Alda was the first to use the term "hán" in Icelandic which is a mix between hann (meaning he) and hún (meaning she).

They became vegan in 2014 as a consequence of the close links between vegan groups and queer groups internationally. As is an emerging pattern, activists for one cause in Iceland tend to be activists for other causes too - and this was a factor.

Alda began baking after becoming a vegan. They describe being able to bake with ease – it came naturally, their mother and grandmother both being great cooks - but not really enjoying this until beginning to make vegan cakes. This also served as useful therapy against depression and PTSD.

They never considered that this could become a business until a former vegan eatery called Kaffi Vínyl advertised for a baker. They got the job but later left as the establishment is no longer vegan. However, baking still sustains them and is a good business. It is an antidote to anxiety, and they consider it a form of mindfulness.

⌃ **Vegan orange cake baked by Alda with freshly grated orange zest on the frosting**

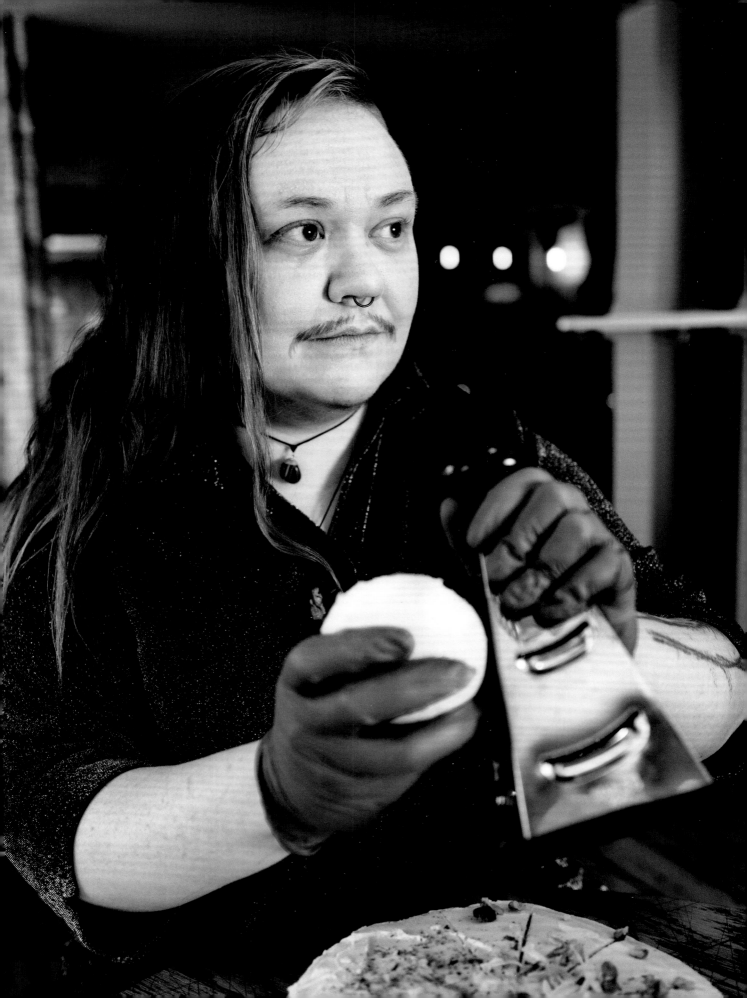

VEGAN PRESIDENT

Benjamin effectively became vegan overnight after losing an argument at a dinner party in 2012. He was elected president of The Icelandic Vegan Society in 2017. It now has over 400 members.

The Society promotes Veganuary each year with an ambitious program including lectures, movie screenings and a political forum. In addition, they provide information, write articles, organise potluck dinners and celebrate a vegan festival each August. They also run annual awards for positive change, with Veganæs, Jömm and Vegan-Búðin having received recognition in recent years.

VEGAN PRESIDENT

» **Linnea Hellström**
Veganæs, Tryggvagata, Reykjavík

VEGAN CHEF

Linnea and her partner Krummi, own Veganæs, a diner inside a "dive bar" in downtown Reykjavík. While this is a venue for rock and roll bands, comedy acts and drag shows, it is also one of the City's finest exclusively vegan eateries.

Originally from Sweden, Linnea, an experienced chef, started cooking professionally in 2007, exclusively using plants. She grew up on a farm, became vegetarian at a young age, and the vegan lifestyle followed soon afterwards. Her motivation was the love of animals and her connection with nature. All the other reasons for being a vegan are a bonus, she says.

Describing herself as an activist, Linnea felt that becoming a chef would be a positive way of demonstrating her activism by offering a practical solution. Having travelled, working with vegan food, and having lived in Spain, Mexico and the USA, she settled in Iceland because it felt like home and

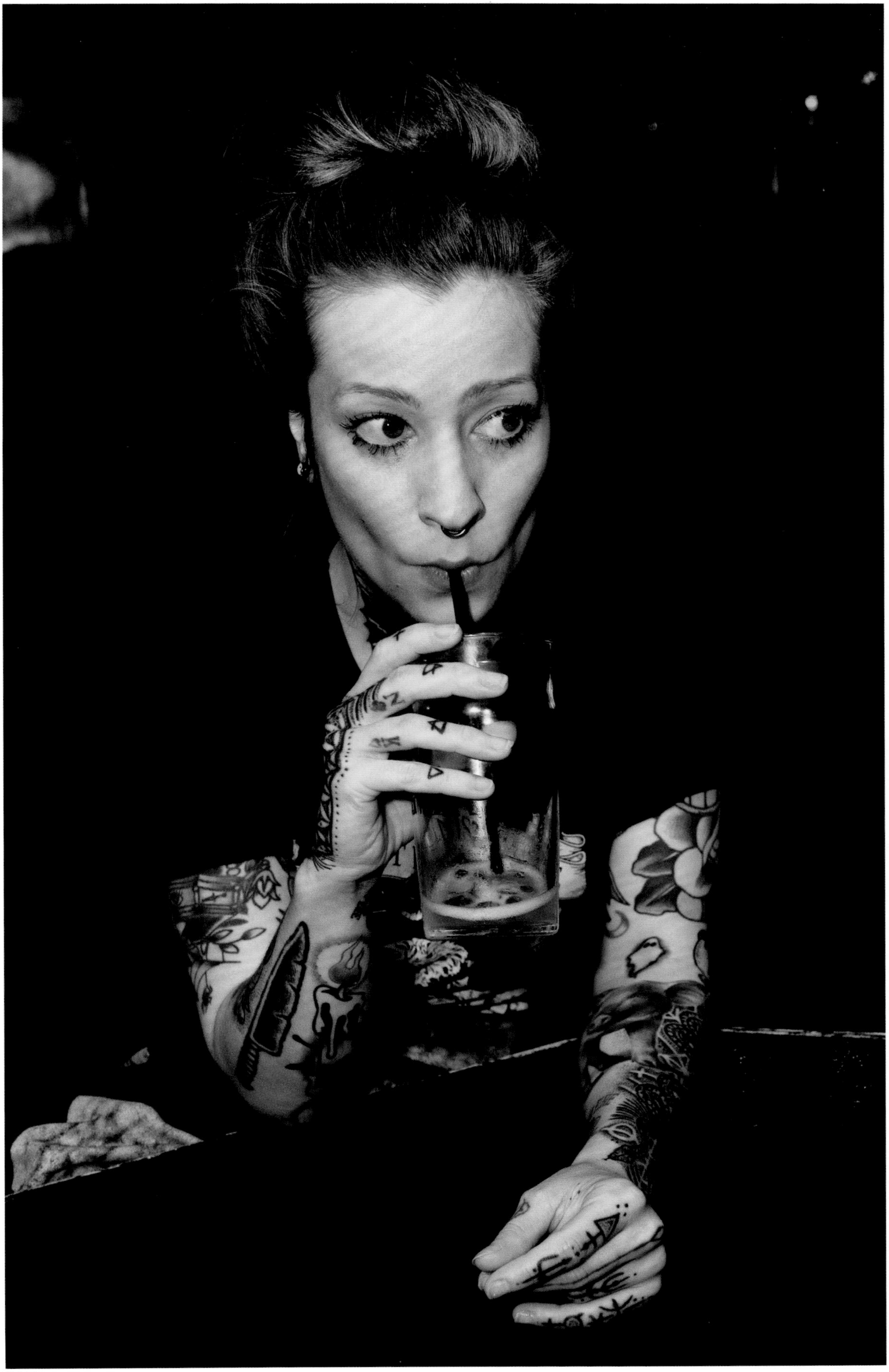

this was the place she had identified as having the greatest need for her great vegan cooking.

Finding an immediate interest in her abilities, she worked as a consulting chef, adding vegan dishes to the menus in many different establishments, trying to spread the word about veganism in this way. For a time, she also worked in the Glo Restaurant and then ran the first all-vegan kitchen in Iceland in 2016, a place called Kaffi Vínyl.

Veganæs was born in 2017, established through a crowdfunding project. When the owners of the current venue became vegan, Linnea and Krummi decided to work with them and open in their space. Other collaborations with non-vegans had not worked out, and they were keen to work with like-minded people. It took a year to build the kitchen, and it opened in the summer of 2018.

Despite appearances, the food is nutritious. Offering burgers, hot dogs, fake steak and pretend fish, the venue is very popular, and the food is delicious. Large portions serve to dispel the myth that vegan fare is not filling. Vegan cheese, as well as the meat substitute, seitan, are all made in house daily. Partner Krummi is also a musician and Linnea successfully influenced him into going vegan too.

Things are now accelerating. Linnea hopes to eventually make a broader range of cruelty-free food to bring to a wider audience in her own space. Bring it on.

VEGAN CHEF

⌄ Pumpkin oatmeal cookies
Joylato, Njálsgata, Reykjavík

VEGAN ART

Styngvi is made up of the first letters of Stefán Yngvi, who is a full-time vegan artist. He and his girlfriend are currently touring Europe in a camper van which doubles up as his studio.

Before taking the plunge into art as a career, Styngvi was working part-time on his distinctive drawings, while programming websites and working as an illustrator.

He has been vegan since moving to The Netherlands in 2014. Alone in a strange city, he felt out of place buying foreign meat and dairy products. His girlfriend was a vegetarian, and they started to explore new recipes together.

It was the film, Cowspiracy, that was the turning point. They became plant-based, initially for the environment. Now being vegan is all-encompassing, and their motivation includes care for animals and a sustainable future.

As part of a student exchange programme, he went to Indonesia. Fortuitously, his sponsor in Indonesia was also vegan, and he and his colleagues cooked their own tofu and tempeh.

⌃ A mug bearing a typical Styngvi illustration
Thor's house

Sticker by Styngvi on a refillable drink bottle
Iceland Air Hotel, Reykjavík Marina

Having drawn since childhood but dropping this while studying, he was inspired to use his skills once again to raise awareness about pollution in the local river. Plastics was his first topic, veganism soon followed.

Feeling that a lot of vegan art was dark and depressing, he was keen to produce something brighter and more optimistic; something that would appeal to a mass audience. He says that because most people love animals, his artwork enables them to make the connection between this and the food they eat.

His artwork is very much in evidence with many Icelandic activists having one or more of his sticker designs.

VEGAN ART

» Elín Skúladóttir with Karen Iva
Hafnarfjörður

VEGAN THERAPY

Elín was diagnosed with breast cancer in 2017 and was prescribed a course of chemotherapy. Her husband had lost his first wife to cancer, and this added to her determination to get better.

Initially, open to anything that would work, she did a lot of research. This quickly indicated that reducing the large amounts of meat and dairy the family consumed might be a good thing. Dairy was immediately ruled out with the household ditching the other animal products soon after.

Elin has since recovered and feels both healthy and empowered by her plant-based and wholefood diet, which involves cooking most things from scratch.

Other family members are now seeing the magic too. Her mother had arthritis,

'My mother had arthritis, and having dropped animal products no longer needs medication. My sister, who could not conceive, has since given birth.'

ELÍN | YOGA TEACHER

and having dropped animal products no longer needs medication. Her sister who could not conceive has since given birth.

These changes have prompted a change in career direction too. Elín recently visited India to learn yoga and now teaches this in addition to her work in finance.

Daughter, Karen Iva, has refused to eat the meat she was offered at school. She has been vegan since birth and wants to keep it that way. Elín says there is great interest in veganism in Iceland. Her example is clearly an inspiration to others.

VEGAN THERAPY

VEGAN MEDIA

A self-confessed media whore, Guðrún presents a daily culture slot on Icelandic TV. Her motivation for being vegan is a love of animals rather than the environment or her health.

Having seen footage from the meat industry, she dreams of being an activist; a voice for the voiceless. Her strategy is to host dinner parties, feeding people delicious vegan food and using her celebrity to raise awareness about veganism.

Guðrún has written a vegan cookery book in Icelandic, *Grænkera Krásir,* which means something like vegan delicacies. She speaks of the book as "mild civil activism" and wishes she had the courage to stand in the street with the other activists. Her inspiration is her dog, which she shares with her parents who live next door.

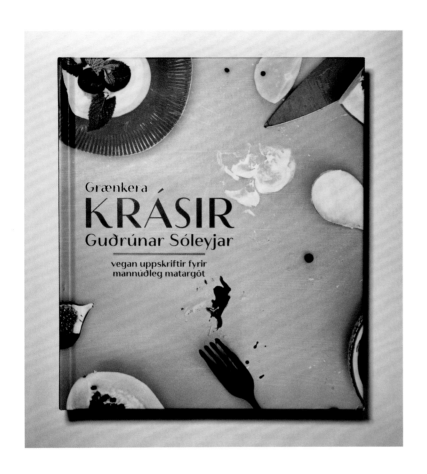

» Sigurður Herlufsen
Tennis and Badminton Club of Reykjavík

VEGAN LEGEND

Sigurður was 83 years old at the time this portrait was taken. He plays table tennis with his friends each week – most of them considerably younger than he is.

He has been vegan for the past 63 years, initially influenced by the Danish philosopher, Martinus Thomsen, generally known as Martinus. In his 1959 work, *The Ideal Food*, Martinus advocated a plant-based diet, something that Sigurður had already embraced by then.

He was married in 1963. He and his wife, are proud that in all the years they have been together, no dead animals have ever entered their kitchen.

Sigurður was responsible for the term grænkeri – the new Icelandic word for vegan.

VEGAN LEGEND

THANKS

I would like to thank everyone who helped make this book possible.

Firstly, Hallgrímar Helgason, although I have not yet met him, for inspiring me to visit Iceland in the first place. Next, Vigga Þórðar, for suggesting so many subjects and for helping to connect me with them.

Thanks too to all the people I photographed, for their warm reception, openness and co-operation. Thank you to those who fed me and to those who kept me company during meals.

Particular thanks are due to Stella Anton for helping me navigate the Icelandic countryside, showing me the hidden beach where the sunk whaling boats are kept and for nearly getting me arrested for putting stickers on joints of meat in a supermarket!

I would also like to thanks Styngvi, whom I missed in Iceland, for taking the trouble to visit my home so that I could get that all-important shot and include him in this work.

Thank you to Abi Read for turning my vision into a credible design and to Gomer Press for the immaculate quality of their printing. And thanks to you, the reader, for supporting the vital work of Sea Shepherd by owning this book.

THANKS

BIOGRAPHY

Dr Jonathan Straight FRSA is a British photographer based in Yorkshire. He specialises in documentary, portrait and street genres. He had no formal training in photography, instead learning at the knee of his late father, who was a keen and talented amateur. Receiving a 35mm camera for his 10th birthday and carefully watching his father work in a home darkroom gave him sufficient grounding to produce his own work.

Having enjoyed a former career as a successful environmental entrepreneur, he now continues to work on various photographic projects as well as being involved with different businesses and charities.

He was shortlisted for the British Portrait Awards 2019, has had photographs published in various places and has held several exhibitions of his work. In 2018, he published *Blood, Sweat, Tears and Helicopters*, a documentary study of the Israeli Ambulance Service. This is his second book of photography.

 @STRAIGHTPIX

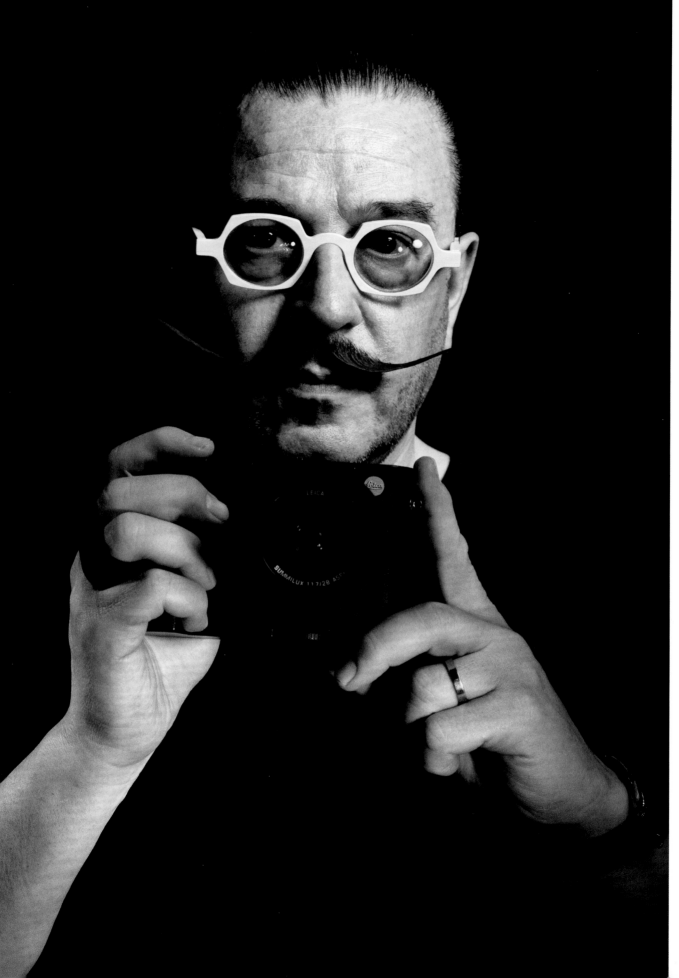

CAMERAS

Leica Q

Fujifilm X100F

iPhone Xs